Gallery Books
Editor: Peter Fallon

THE MAN WHO WAS
MARKED BY WINTER

Paula Meehan

THE MAN WHO WAS MARKED BY WINTER

For Nancy

with a warm

welcome to Dublin

in August 1994

Paula x

Gallery Books

The Man who was Marked by Winter
was first published
simultaneously in paperback
and in a clothbound edition
in May 1991.
Reprinted 1992, 1994.

The Gallery Press
Loughcrew
Oldcastle
County Meath
Ireland

ISBN 1 85235 071 7 (*paperback*)
     1 85235 072 5 (*clothbound*)

The Gallery Press receives financial assistance from An Chomhairle
Ealaíon / The Arts Council, Ireland.

Contents

Acknowledgements

Some of these poems or versions of them first appeared in the following publications: *The Sunday Tribune, Evening Herald, The Connacht Tribune, Krino, Poetry Ireland Review, Cyphers, Stet, ACE Poetry Broadsheet, Willow Springs, The Globe, Inner City Magazine, Poets for Africa, Counting Backward, The Great Book of Ireland, Wildish Things* (Attic Press) and *W. B. Yeats International Theatre Festival Pamphlet*, 1990. Some, in different forms, were published in *Return and No Blame* (1984) and *Reading the Sky* (1986) published by Beaver Row Press. Some of these poems or versions of them were broadcast on RTE radio and television, Christian Science Monitor Broadcasting Service and National Public Broadcasting (US).

Acknowledgements are also due to The Arts Council/An Chomhairle Ealaíon for a Bursary in Literature which kept many wolves from the door while these poems were being made.

for Tony Cafferky

Blessed be the road that does not end.
Blessed be each minute that borrows us
To witness its eternity.

We are old: a species gone to seed,
Run wild under the stars;
And our talk is old talk

While we watch our brazen children
Clutch at memory of when the land
Was waking to a young and lusty sun.

The Leaving

He had fallen so far down into himself
I couldn't reach him.
Though I had arranged our escape
he wouldn't budge. He sat
days in his room checking manuscripts

or fixing photos of his family
strictly in the order they were taken.
I begged him hurry for
the moonless nights were due;
it was two nights' walk through the forest.

The soldiers had recently entered our quarter.
I dreaded each knock on the door,
their heavy boots on the stairs.
Our friends advised haste;
many neighbours were already in prison.

His eyes were twin suns burning.
Silence was his answer to my pleas.
I packed a change of clothes, half
the remaining rations,
my mother's gold ring for barter.

The documents at a glance would pass.
It wasn't for myself I went but
for the new life I carried.
At the frontier I recalled him — that last morning
by the window watching the sun

strut the length of the street, mirroring
the clouds' parade. He wore
the black shirt I'd embroidered with stars
and said nothing. Nothing.
Then the guide pushed me forward.

Between one sweep of the searchlight
and the next, I slipped into another state
gratefully, under cover of darkness.

Her Dream

This is the fountain. You could overlook it
from a balcony. I would cup
cool water under the moon's reflection
occluding the lines on my palm.

I would carry this small moon for you
through the city's narrow streets, through
blighted raging days to fling it at your feet:
a spent coin thrown down on cobbles.

I would wear a white dress edged with poppies,
I would pin golden rings in my ears
and walk the edge of the fountain round
to spin you a fatal story.

The square would be bereft of chanting
children, of men at games of chess,
of women bearing home goods from market
and cats who ought be napping on the sills.

My thirteen plots are all the same.
I borrow all my maps.

Zugzwang

She fills jugs of water at the sink
for flowers: mignonette, cotton lavender,
for their scent and fretty form,
sweet pea and love-lies-bleeding,
a token of domestic tragedy, a wound.

He looks up from the chessboard where
he's replaying a famous game of Capablanca's.
He catches her off guard, murmuring
to herself, framed by the door, the blooms.
She wears a dress for a change,
of a sea blue that ebbs to green
when sun floods the kitchen.
Beyond is the window. The sky is an ocean
where clouds like spacecraft or cuban cigars
float towards the mountain.
He imagines Dutch paintings, bourgeois
interiors, *Woman Washing*, *Woman Setting
a Table*, *Woman Bending over a Child*
and conjures a painting half made —
Woman Surrounded by Flowers at a Sink,
himself at an easel mixing pigment and oil,
a north facing studio above a canal
where barges are waiting their turn at the lock
and on the Zuyder Zee scuppy waves rock sailboats.
The landscape surrenders to a polar light.

She arranges the flowers in two jugs.
Lately she has heard her dead mother's voice
tumbling in the drier with the wash:

I told you so, I told you so, I told you so.
The women on the TV in their business suits
and white teeth transmit coded messages,
escape maps buried in their speeches,
though they appear to be reading the news
lest others are watching. Soldiers
have set up a barricade down the road;
they are part of a nationwide search
for a desperate man and his hostage.

A jug in each hand, she moves to the table
and he fancies she has stepped straight into
a Cretan mosaic, a priestess in a Minoan rite,
devotee of the bull, and himself a mosaic worker
fingering a thousand fragments until he finds
the exact shade of blue with that green undertow
to fit his pattern. For her face
and breasts he would use tiles of pure gold;
the alchemists hold it has the exact
calibration of human skin. He will not dwell

on last week's events when he woke
in the night and she was gone. He found her
digging in the garden, her nightgown
drenched through, muck smeared on her arms,
on her legs, the rain lashing down.
She explained that she wanted to be close
to her loved ones, her lost ones, that
they are so cold and lonely in the earth
and they long for the warmth of the living.

She places the flowers on the table.
Any day now she will let go her grip,
surrender herself to the ecstatic freefall.

We are all aware that when she hits bottom
she will shatter into smithereens.
Each shard will reflect the room, the flowers,
the chessboard, and her beloved sky beyond
like a calm ocean lapping at the mountain.

Buying Winkles

My mother would spare me sixpence and say,
'Hurry up now and don't be talking to strange
men on the way.' I'd dash from the ghosts
on the stairs where the bulb had blown
out into Gardiner Street, all relief.
A bonus if the moon was in the strip of sky
between the tall houses, or stars out,
but even in rain I was happy — the winkles
would be wet and glisten blue like little
night skies themselves. I'd hold the tanner tight
and jump every crack in the pavement,
I'd wave up to women at sills or those
lingering in doorways and weave a glad path through
men heading out for the night.

She'd be sitting outside the Rosebowl Bar
on an orange-crate, a pram loaded
with pails of winkles before her.
When the bar doors swung open they'd leak
the smell of men together with drink
and I'd see light in golden mirrors.
I envied each soul in the hot interior.

I'd ask her again to show me the right way
to do *it*. She'd take a pin from her shawl —
'Open the eyelid. So. Stick it in
till you feel a grip, then slither him out.
Gently, mind.' The sweetest extra winkle

that brought the sea to me.
'Tell yer Ma I picked them fresh this morning.'

I'd bear the newspaper twists
bulging fat with winkles
proudly home, like torches.

The Pattern

Little has come down to me of hers,
a sewing machine, a wedding band,
a clutch of photos, the sting of her hand
across my face in one of our wars

when we had grown bitter and apart.
Some say that's the fate of the eldest daughter.
I wish now she'd lasted till after
I'd grown up. We might have made a new start

as women without tags like *mother*, *wife*,
sister, *daughter*, taken our chances from there.
At forty-two she headed for god knows where.
I've never gone back to visit her grave.

❧ ❧

First she'd scrub the floor with Sunlight soap,
an armreach at a time. When her knees grew sore
she'd break for a cup of tea, then start again
at the door with lavender polish. The smell
would percolate back through the flat to us,
her brood banished to the bedroom.

And as she buffed the wax to a high shine
did she catch her own face coming clear?
Did she net a glimmer of her true self?
Did her mirror tell what mine tells me?

I have her shrug and go on
knowing history has brought her to her knees.

She'd call us in and let us skate around
in our socks. We'd grow solemn as planets
in an intricate orbit about her.

ᘒ ᘓ

She's bending over crimson cloth,
the younger kids are long in bed.
Late summer, cold enough for a fire,
she works by fading light
to remake an old dress for me.
It's first day back at school tomorrow.

ᘒ ᘓ

'Pure lambswool. Plenty of wear in it yet.
You know I wore this when I went out with your Da.
I was supposed to be down in a friend's house,
your Granda caught us at the corner.
He dragged me in by the hair — it was long as yours then —
in front of the whole street.
He called your Da every name under the sun,
cornerboy, lout; I needn't tell you
what he called me. He shoved my whole head
under the kitchen tap, took a scrubbing brush
and carbolic soap and in ice-cold water he scrubbed
every spick of lipstick and mascara off my face.
Christ but he was a right tyrant, your Granda.
It'll be over my dead body anyone harms a hair
    of your head.'

She must have stayed up half the night
to finish the dress. I found it airing at the fire,
three new copybooks on the table and a bright
bronze nib, St. Christopher strung on a silver wire,

as if I were embarking on a perilous journey
to uncharted realms. I wore that dress
with little grace. To me it spelt poverty,
the stigma of the second hand. I grew enough to pass

it on by Christmas to the next in line. I was sizing
up the world beyond our flat patch by patch
daily after school, and fitting each surprising
city street to city square to diamond. I'd watch

the Liffey for hours pulsing to the sea
and the coming and going of ships,
certain that one day it would carry me
to Zanzibar, Bombay, the Land of the Ethiops.

❧ ❧

There's a photo of her taken in the Phoenix Park
alone on a bench surrounded by roses
as if she had been born to formal gardens.
She stares out as if unaware
that any human hand held the camera, wrapped
entirely in her own shadow, the world beyond her
already a dream, already lost. She's
eight months pregnant. Her last child.

Her steel needles sparked and clacked,
the only other sound a settling coal
or her sporadic mutter
at a hard part in the pattern.
She favoured sensible shades:
Moss Green, Mustard, Beige.

I dreamt a robe of a colour
so pure it became a word.

Sometimes I'd have to kneel
an hour before her by the fire,
a skein around my outstretched hands,
while she rolled wool into balls.
If I swam like a kite too high
amongst the shadows on the ceiling
or flew like a fish in the pools
of pulsing light, she'd reel me firmly
home, she'd land me at her knees.

Tongues of flame in her dark eyes,
she'd say, 'One of these days I must
teach you to follow a pattern.'

Ard Fheis

Down through the cigarette smoke
the high windows cast
ecstatic light to the floorboards
stiletto pocked and butt scorched

but now such golden pools of sun to bask in there.
I am fish
water my demesne.
The room pulses in, then out, of focus

and all this talk of the people, of who we are,
of what we need, is robbed of meaning,
becomes sub-melody, sonic undertow,
a room of children chanting off

by heart a verse. I'm nine or ten,
the Central Model School,
Miss Shannon beats out the metre
with her stick.

I wind up in the ghost place
the language rocks me to,
a cobwebby state, chilled vault
littered with our totems;

a tattered Starry Plough,
a bloodstained Proclamation,
Connolly strapped wounded to a chair,
May blossom in Kilmainham.

I am following my father's steps
on a rainy Sunday in the National Museum,
by talisman of torc, carved spiral,
síle na gig's yoni made luscious in stone.

And somewhere there is vestige
of my mother nursing me to sleep,
when all my world was touch,
and possibly was peace.

I float down to a September evening,
the Pro-Cathedral, girls in rows at prayer,
gaze at the monstrance, lulled to adoration,
mesmeric in frankincense and candlelight:

Hail our life our sweetness and our hope
to thee do we cry poor banished children of Eve
to thee do we send up our sighs
mourning and weeping in this valley of tears.

I push back to the surface, break clear,
the light has come on fluorescent
and banishes my dreaming self.
It is, after all, an ordinary room

and we are ordinary people.
We pull our collars up and head
for the new moon sky of our city
fondling each whorled bead in our macabre rosary.

Don't even speak to me of Stephen the Martyr,
the host snug in his palm,
slipping through the wounded streets
to keep his secret safe.

Return and No Blame

Father of mine,
your sunny smile
is a dandelion
as I come once again through the door.

Our fumbled embrace
drives the wind off my shoulder
and your eyes hold a question
you will not put
as I break bread at your table
after the long seasons away from it.

Father, my head is bursting
with the things I've seen
in this strange, big world

but I don't have the words to tell you
nor the boldness to disrupt your gentle daily ways,
so I am quiet while the rashers cook,
nod and grin at any old thing.

'Oh, the boat was grand,
they took me in at Larne.'
'And a pity they didn't keep you.
Must have been a gypsy slipped you in
and I in a dead sleep one night.'

Didn't I rob you of your eyes, father,
and her of her smile? No dark blood
but the simple need to lose an uneasy love

drove me down unknown roads
where they spoke in different tongues,
drove me about the planet
till I had of it
and it of me
what we needed of each other.

Yes, father, I will have more tea
and sit here quiet in this room of my childhood
and watch while the flames flicker
the story of our distance on the wall.

Two Buck Tim from Timbuctoo

I found it in the granary under rubble
where the back gable caved in,
a 78 miraculously whole in a nest of smashed records,
as if it had been hatched by a surreal hen,
a pullet with a taste for the exotic.

I took it in and swabbed it down,
put it on the turntable and filled the cottage
with its scratchy din. Ghosts of the long dead
flocked from their narrow grooves beneath foreign soils
to foxtrot round my kitchen in the dusk.

I'd say Leitrim in the forties was every bit as depressed
as Leitrim is today, the young were heading off
in droves, the same rain fell all winter long.
Eventually one old woman was left looking at her hands
while the Bell Boys of Broadway played 'Two Buck Tim from
    Timbuctoo',

and dreamt her daughters back about the place, the swing of a
    skirt,
a face caught in lamplight, with every revolution of the disc.
This winter I have grown unduly broody. As I go
about my daily work an otherworldly mantra turns
within my head: Two Buck Tim from Timbuctoo,

Two Buck Tim from Timbuctoo. It keeps me up at night.
I roam about the rooms. I hope to catch them at it.
I want to rend the veil, step out onto their plane,
spiral down a rain-washed road, let some ghostly partner
take the lead, become at last another migrant soul.

Reading the Sky

We stood in the still pine shadows
with nightshade and yarrow
and read the cyphers the wild geese drew

across the violet sky.
Go south, go south, they insisted,
winter is close behind.

The moon was for a moment
a perfect golden sickle
above the golden lake.

We measured the angles of the stars
revealed by the dwindling light
and gave to them new names

learned from the geese in flight
knowing that one would follow,
one would be left behind.

We glean a common language
to describe our differing fates:
you'll be fugitive forever,

I'll wait at the brink of winter
holding off the dark
that you may escape.

Elegy for a Child

It is not that the spring brings
you back. Birds riotous about
the house, fledglings learn to fly.

Nor that coming on petals drifted in the orchard
is like opening your door, a draught of pastel,
a magpie hoard of useless bright.

Clouds move over the river
under the sun — a cotton sheet shook out.
The pines bring me news
from deeper in the woods:
the rain will come sing on the roof soon.

It is not the day's work in the garden,
the seedlings neatly leafmould mulched in lines.
Not the woodpile trim bespeaking good husbandry,
conjuring up the might-have-been.

It is not the anarchic stream
in a stone-sucking dash past the crane's haunt, fickle,
sky mirror now, now shattered bauble,

nor the knowledge of planets in proper order,
their passage through my fourth house
fixed before I was born.
It is not that the night you died
a star plummeted to earth.
It is not that I watched it fall.

It is not that I was your mother,
nor the rooted deep down loss,
that has brought me this moment
to sit by the window and weep.

You were but a small bird balanced
within me
ready for flight.

Child Burial

Your coffin looked unreal,
fancy as a wedding cake.

I chose your grave clothes with care,
your favourite stripey shirt,

your blue cotton trousers.
They smelt of woodsmoke, of October,

your own smell there too.
I chose a gansy of handspun wool,

warm and fleecy for you. It is
so cold down in the dark.

No light can reach you and teach you
the paths of wild birds,

the names of the flowers,
the fishes, the creatures.

Ignorant you must remain
of the sun and its work,

my lamb, my calf, my eaglet,
my cub, my kid, my nestling,

my suckling, my colt. I would spin
time back, take you again

within my womb, your amniotic lair,
and further spin you back

through nine waxing months
to the split seeding moment

you chose to be made flesh,
word within me.

I'd cancel the love feast
the hot night of your making.

I would travel alone
to a quiet mossy place,

you would spill from me into the earth
drop by bright red drop.

No Go Area

In the first zone
you will be stripped and searched
for hidden weapons.

In the second zone
you must know their language
or they'll finger you as other.

In the third zone
bribe the guard — it's quicker.
The beast is quite tame by day.

In the fourth zone
an oxygen mask is mandatory.
That's where they stack the bodies.

In the fifth zone
it's all sex and experiments.
Few ever go this far.

In the sixth zone
you will have trouble in the dark
knowing if you're beast or offering.

In the seventh zone
stands the gate to the no go area.
Go, God help you, there you're on your own.

Her Heroin Dream

She dreamt the moon a gaudy egg,
a Chinese gimcrack. When it hatched,
a young dragon would spiral to earth
trailing garnet and emerald sparks,
shrieking through the ozone layer,
the citizens blinded by dragon-glory.

In the heart of night would blaze a light
greater than the sun, supernova fierce.

The Liffey and the two canals would vanish
and Dublin bay evaporate, leaving beached
spiny prawns and crabs, coiled sea snails,
a dead sailor's shoe, shipping wrecks,
radioactive waste in Saharas of sand.
The buildings would scorch to black stumps,
windows melt, railroads buckle,
bricks fallen to dust would sift
in dervish swirls along the thoroughfares.

Each tree in the town would turn torch
to celebrate his passing.

She would wait in her cell.
He'd enter softly in the guise of a youth:
his eyes the blue of hyacinth,
his skin like valerian,
his lips Parthian red.
He'd take her from behind.

The kundalini energy would shoot straight up her spine,
blow her head open like a flower.
Dragon seed would root deep in her womb.
Dragon nature course through her veins.

They'd slip from the cell hands twined,
glide over the prison wall into a new morning
to sport among the ruins.

The Man who Lives in the Clouds

You said if we reached the top
we'd find the navel of the earth,
proof that matter was a mere prop,
a gift, our right from birth,

to keep us occupied through time,
that energy alone was real.
I was breathless from the climb.
I wanted a bed and a decent meal.

I was sick of the dirt, the reek of yak
butter seeping from my haversack,
the prospect of another night,
the endless talk of humanity's plight,

of philosophers' stones and holy grails.
I wanted nothing more than to stand
humbly on the lower slopes and gaze
at the peaks, and whether I was damned

or saved was much of a muchness to me.
You claimed the dead lived deep inside
the mountain, that they clamoured to be free.
I heard only the wind lash like a tide

race through the trees. I left
you then and made for home, deaf
to your threats, your curses. Now
I lead a quiet life in the village below.

I've a clutch of hens, a herb patch, a video
and a black cat. I do not think of you
up there with your yetis, your eagles, your thunderbolts,
and your dense cloud cover the sun can't break through.

The Dark Twin

You believe
they contract when you turn to the window —
there's a girl in pink passing
you might or might not know
down a street you say history will be made on
as the woman you hold turns to your eyes.
Anemones, she tells you, make the same sound as pupils.
Pishew, *pishew*, were you close enough
in rockpool silence, is what you'd hear.

And you believe
she'll turn again and again to your eyes
as you hold her. Show your stored wisdom
in a ritual of healing. Your hands move
over her dark form. She can't refuse you.
Gulls cross the sky, bells sound for first Mass.
You know she'll seek you for she is
your dark twin. Her eyes don't reflect you.
Her pupils are still as the dark pool
she grew from. She names you *diablo*.
If you enter her now you can teach her
the nature of history, the city that's made her.
She'll name a price later and say you've had
her cheaply. She'll be just. You won't haggle
but find the exact change and count it into her palm.

And you believe
she'll return and desire you once more —
more than her own life, more than her darkness.

This you know surely as you glance over
her eyes to the girl in pink passing.
You move above her: by your ritual rocking
you'll move her to tears.
She'll learn to accept love though still
you must pay her the exact amount due.

And you believe
you can quieten her sobs in the morning
when she tells you again
how the world will succumb to men in dark uniforms.
You believe she has stood, her face to a stone wall,
while the men cock their rifles and wait for the order.
You know she's been there. You know you can heal her.
She is your dark twin. You know you must heal her.
The burns from the bombings will ease as you rock her.
The legs that are mangled made whole for fast dancing.
Her sobs will be songs for the rearing of children.
Still you must pay her the exact amount due.

And you believe all this
as you turn from the window,
the girl in pink passing at the moment
you enter your dark twin. Your pupils
dilate, your breath as it leaves you
makes the one word you can never repay her.

Lullaby

for Brenda Meehan

My sister is sleeping
and makes small murmurs
as she turns in a dream

she is swinging a child
under the shade of
a lilac tree blooming

in a garden in springtime
my sister is sleeping.

The rain falls
on Finglas
to each black roof

it lashes a story
of time on the ocean
of moon on the river

and flashes down drainpipes
into deep gutters.

My sister is sleeping
her hands full of blossoms
plucked for the child

who dreams in her womb
rocked in tall branches
close to the stars

where my sister is sleeping
within her small child.

The Statue of the Virgin
at Granard Speaks

It can be bitter here at times like this,
November wind sweeping across the border.
Its seeds of ice would cut you to the quick.
The whole town tucked up safe and dreaming,
even wild things gone to earth, and I
stuck up here in this grotto, without as much as
star or planet to ease my vigil.

The howling won't let up. Trees
cavort in agony as if they would be free
and take off — ghost voyagers
on the wind that carries intimations
of garrison towns, walled cities, ghetto lanes
where men hunt each other and invoke
the various names of God as blessing
on their death tactics, their night manoeuvres.
Closer to home the wind sails over
dying lakes. I hear fish drowning.
I taste the stagnant water mingled
with turf smoke from outlying farms.

They call me Mary — Blessed, Holy, Virgin.
They fit me to a myth of a man crucified:
the scourging and the falling, and the falling again,
the thorny crown, the hammer blow of iron
into wrist and ankle, the sacred bleeding heart.

They name me Mother of all this grief
though mated to no mortal man.
They kneel before me and their prayers
fly up like sparks from a bonfire
that blaze a moment, then wink out.

It can be lovely here at times. Springtime,
early summer. Girls in Communion frocks
pale rivals to the riot in the hedgerows
of cow parsley and haw blossom, the perfume
from every rushy acre that's left for hay
when the light swings longer with the sun's push north.

Or the grace of a midsummer wedding
when the earth herself calls out for coupling
and I would break loose of my stony robes,
pure blue, pure white, as if they had robbed
a child's sky for their colour. My being
cries out to be incarnate, incarnate,
maculate and tousled in a honeyed bed.

Even an autumn burial can work its own pageantry.
The hedges heavy with the burden of fruiting
crab, sloe, berry, hip; clouds scud east
pear scented, windfalls secret in long
orchard grasses, and some old soul is lowered
to his kin. Death is just another harvest
scripted to the season's play.

But on this All Souls' Night there is
no respite from the keening of the wind.
I would not be amazed if every corpse came risen
from the graveyard to join in exaltation with the gale,

a cacophony of bone imploring sky for judgement
and release from being the conscience of the town.

On a night like this I remember the child
who came with fifteen summers to her name,
and she lay down alone at my feet
without midwife or doctor or friend to hold her hand
and she pushed her secret out into the night,
far from the town tucked up in little scandals,
bargains struck, words broken, prayers, promises,
and though she cried out to me in extremis
I did not move,
I didn't lift a finger to help her,
I didn't intercede with heaven,
nor whisper the charmed word in God's ear.

On a night like this I number the days to the solstice
and the turn back to the light.
                              O sun,
centre of our foolish dance,
burning heart of stone,
molten mother of us all,
hear me and have pity.

Fruit

Alone in the room
with the statue of Venus
I couldn't resist
cupping her breast.

It was cool
and heavy in my hand
like an apple.

Night Walk: Effernagh to Eslin

Earth shadows the moon,
leaves just a paring
of light to get home by.

You follow iced potholes
that gleam in the dark,
pebbles, perhaps, dropped by a child

when her father and mother
have left her to find her
own way out of the forest.

A stream weeps. The lake
past blackthorn hedges
is waiting for *finder*

to keep her. And you
still have three miles to go,
three miles to go and

no promise of sleep, but
the long night vigil
and drowning in pools

that go down forever
and there's no way out
and the bottom is never.

Mist grazes a meadow,
spills through a gap
to fresh pasture.

You have to get home.
Someone is waiting.
The table is set.

The kettle near boiling,
the clock ticks louder.
He paces the floor

from chair to window,
sees nothing outside
but himself looking in.

At the top of the hill
you make out a light
between pine and willow.

The last mile it measures
your step on the road,
human in the darkness.

Home by Starlight

for Lisa Steppe

You ask me which I prefer —
the stars themselves or their mirror
image on the puddles of our path
home. Their light as strong
as moonlight, the night cold and still.
We take a shortcut across an overgrown rath,
old stones that seem to spill
haphazardly, but if you haul back the long
ivy tendrils, hack through the brambles, you
will find patterns there, you

will know lifetimes ago we gazed
at the same constellations amazed
by such brilliance, and found in their rule
the measure of each year, each journey.
Do you remember how it was?
The seasons of study in the star school
scanning for portent conjugations
of sky beasts which peopled the sea
of our heavens. Do you remember
that crazy light we tracked one mid-winter?

The light they later called the Christos,
and the terror, the blood cost of that Logos?
How our arts were eclipsed and many
gentle comrades tortured and burned?

How the songs we had crafted for travel
were lost, language itself lost, when we
were scattered like sparks to the wind? So well
you might ask — the light, or its image, turned
in a puddle, surefooted friend on the path you roam
by the light of a million million suns home.

You Open Your Hands to Me

They hold nothing
They are calloused
Earth under the fingernails
The heart line strong and sure
As any river crazy for the sea

These hands hold nothing
They are the hands of a worker
They are the hands of one who has no job

They have tucked a whole city up at night
And in the morning cast it adrift

These hands could pack everything they value
In a minute or less

From a burning building
They would save what is living
Not what is Art

They reach to me in the dark
Of a nightmare
They pull me clear
They place the particular stars I prefer
At my window
On cloudy nights
They make images of the moon
In case I am lonely

These hands hold nothing
They do not judge
They are drawn to the wounded
They have no history
They fire the first shot

They are the hands of a builder
They dismantle empires
They love most what is wild
They invite no pity

Were I dying I would choose
These hands to guide me
Out of the world

You open your hands to me
Your empty hands

Coda

You open the hated book,
the book of my self.
The more that you read there
the fainter the print becomes
until the letters are faded,
white nests protected by the page.

I gave up on the window box:
leaves went transparent,
eaten away by greenfly.
When you come home you'll find
geranium ghosts, spectral nasturtiums,
a flock of albino butterflies
settled on the sill. I'll be hung

up in the larder by the heels,
dressed as a deer would be,
my skin in a casual heap on the floor.
You can wear it if you wish
though flesh clings to parts,
especially the extremities. Still,
a sharp flint stone could do the trick.

It should be a comfortable fit.
There's a note in the dresser
on French seams and buttonholes
lest you need to alter any part.
The breasts will be a problem;

you'll need the smallest crewel for the job
and the good new scissors of German steel.
The offcuts may be useful somewhere else.

Put the rest of me on at gas mark 3,
(you know those stringy muscles in my back!).
Don't forget to baste me now and then.
Don't bring your current lover home to tea,
there's just enough for one. Besides
I'm an acquired taste, like squid
or pickled limes. I wouldn't delay —
were I you I'd catch the earliest ferry
else the worms will have their way with me.

You'd come upon me bleached and empty
in the cool larder rafters, the slates blown down,
green garden light nesting in my bones.

The Man who was Marked
  by Winter

He was heading for Bridal Veil Falls,
an upward slog on a dusty path.
Mid May and hot as a mill-

stone grinding his shoulders, his back.
Each breath was a drowning.
And who's to say if it was a mirage

the other side of the creek's brown
water. He saw it, that's enough,
in the deep shade of a rocky overhang —

the spoor of winter, a tracery of ice. If
we'd reached him, we'd have warned him of the depth,
the secret current underneath.

He must have been half crazy with the heat.
He stripped off. Waded in.
His feet were cut from under him. He was swept

downriver in melt water from the mountain.
She clutched him to her breast, that beast of winter.
One look from her agate eyes and he abandoned

hope. He was pliant. She pulled him under.
If she had him once, she had him thrice.
She shook his heart and mind asunder.

And he would willingly have gone back to her palace
or her lair, whichever; whatever she was,
he would have lived forever in her realms of ice.

She must have grown tired of his human ways.
We found him tossed like a scrap on the bank,
hours or years or seconds later. His eyes

stared straight at the sun. His past is a blank
snowfield where no one will step. She made her mark
below his heart, a five-fingered gash — *Bondsman.*

Insomnia

Pale under the moon
through the glass
his limbs still
and soon
before stormclouds pass
over the house and fill

it with darkness she'll slip
in beside him
as into a pool.
Warm ripples will lap
her thighs, brim
her breasts, spool

her close and free
her mind of the trouble
that has kept her late
by the fire, a fragrancy
of applewood, to struggle
with her fate

which has always been
to leave what is familiar,
trusted, known,
for the half-seen
shadow world, far
beyond the human zone.

Three Paintings of York Street

for Ita Kelly

Before the Pubs Close

Quick. Before the moon is eaten
by that cloud, rescue its dust,
sift it over the shopping centre,
the student hostel, that couple
hand in hand walking to the Green.
And quick. Before last orders and drunken cries
steal the breath the street is holding,
exhale it lovingly below each window
to reclaim from night the shadowy areas.

Salt your canvas with a woman
quietly weeping in a tenement room
until her tears become a blessing
sprinkled from your fingers,
those spatters of intense blue
beside the three black cats
who wait with . . . patience, is it?,
on a granite step for you to find
the exact amber of their eyes
as they gaze at the moon.

Woman Found Dead behind Salvation Army Hostel

You will have to go outside for this one.
The night is bitter cold
but you must go out,
you could not invent this.

You can make a quick sketch
and later, in your studio, mix the colours,
the purple, the eerie green of her bruises,
the garish crimson of her broken mouth.

For consolation there's the line
her spine makes as it remembers
its beginnings, as if at the very end
she turned foetal and knew again
the roar of her mother's blood in her ears,
the drum of her mother's heart
before she drowned in the seventh wave
beyond pain, or your pity.

Your hand will steady as you draw the cobbles.
They impose a discipline, the comfort of habit,
as does the symmetry of brick walls
which define the alley and whose very height
cut off the light and hid
the beast who maimed her.

Children of York Street at Play in the College of Surgeons' Carpark

You worry given the subject
about sentimentality, about indulgence,
but as you work
the children turn to pattern
and you may as well be
weaving in a Turkish bazaar, one eye
on your son lest he topple to the tarmac.
And your fingers of their own volition
find the perfect stress between warp and weft.
Your mind can lope as loosely
as a gazelle through savannah
or nimble as a mountain goat,
attain an unexpected purchase on a sheer
cliff face, or you may be dolphin
and cavort the prismatic ranges
of the green sea's depth.
                              And after,
cleaning brushes, you will wonder
why no child can be discerned
on your canvas, why there is no bike,
no skateboard, no skipping rope,
no carpark, why your colours are
all primary, pure as you can make them,
why in your pattern the shapes keep shifting
like flighty spirits threatening
to burst into song.

My Love about his Business in the Barn

You're fiddling with something in the barn,
a makeshift yoke for beans to climb,
held together like much in our lives
with blue baling twine, scraps of chicken wire.

Such a useless handyman: our world could collapse,
frequently *has* with a huff and a puff.
You'd hoke a length of string from your back pocket,
humming a Woody Guthrie song, you'd bind

the lintel to stone, the slate to rafter,
'It'll do for the minute if the wind stays down.'
And so I've learned to live with dodgy matter:
shelves that tumble to the floor if you glance

at them sideways; walls that were not built
for leaning against; a great chasm in the kitchen
crossable only by a rope bridge; a blow hole
by our bed where the Atlantic spouts.

On stormy nights it drenches the walls, the ceiling.
Days you come home reeking of *Brut* and brimstone
I suspect you've been philandering underground
and not breaking your back beyond on the bog.

So is it any wonder when I see you
mooching in the barn this fine May morning,
a charm of finches lending local colour,
that I rush for my holy water, my rabbit's foot?

That I shut my eyes tight and wait
for the explosion, then the silence,
then the sweet aftershock when the earth skids
under me, when stars and deep space usurp my day?

Mysteries of the Home

The soul stands, lonely in its choice,
Waiting, itself a slow thing,
In the changing body.
                   — Theodore Roethke

Well

I know this path by magic not by sight.
Behind me on the hillside the cottage light
is like a star that's gone astray. The moon
is waning fast, each blade of grass a rune
inscribed by hoarfrost. This path's well worn.
I lug a bucket by bramble and blossoming blackthorn.
I know this path by magic not by sight.
Next morning when I come home quite unkempt
I cannot tell what happened at the well.
You spurn my explanation of a sex spell
cast by the spirit who guards the source
that boils deep in the belly of the earth,
even when I show you what lies strewn
in my bucket — a golden waning moon,
seven silver stars, our own porch light,
your face at the window staring into the dark.

Queen

Go then. Don't let me stand in your way.
I hope you'll be very happy. She's quite
pretty if you like that type. Not a hair astray,
all that jangly jewellery, teeth so white
and even. Are they real? She's like a queen,
you a subject yoked to plod her wake.
I who spurn vanity admit
a fascination with her nails, long, sharp,
red as rosehips flashing in autumn dusk.
That dress — lotus flowers on a field of green,
just the thing to swan around your bedsit
in. Forgive me if I harp.
I never meant to nag you, act the wife,
it's just your cringing wounds me like a knife.

Hermit

I'll go out into the world now.
If I meet a snake I'll charm it.
It'll wind round my staff and grow
timid as a lamb. I'll keep
some books and work by night for choice.
You can have the daily kingdom,
you can have the pots, the pans, the sheets,
you can have the home, the garden.
My body will be my shelter. I'll
keel off like a snail. If
on a moonlit night you see my glistening tracks
and are overcome by remorse — tough.
I'll survive on air and scholarship
and the delight of my own voice

making songs and prayers
and, if I'm greatly blessed, a poem or two.

King

When I came to your inner chamber
having fought through the ranks of shadowy petitioners
you gave me the glad eye and sent
a note by a trusted courtier.
You promised a life of ease,
a place to work in peace,
songbirds and panthers, never
a worry about where the next meal was coming from,
no more hiding from the rent man, the ESB man,
the wolfman gnawing at my door.
And when you had me, burned me out,
you placed my ashes in your collection.
Number 8. A fine woman.
Pity about her accent though.

Seed

The first warm day of spring
and I step out into the garden from the gloom
of a house where hope had died
to tally the storm damage, to seek what may
have survived. And finding some forgotten
lupins I'd sown from seed last autumn
holding in their fingers a raindrop each
like a peace offering, or a promise,
I am suddenly grateful and would
offer a prayer if I believed in God.
But not believing, I bless the power of seed,
its casual, useful persistence,
and bless the power of sun,
its conspiracy with the underground,
and thank my stars the winter's ended.